PIANO SOLO

TOMORROWLAND

ISBN 978-1-4950-2990-5

Wonderland Music Company, Inc.
Walt Disney Music Company

DISTRIBUTED BY

7777 W. BLUEMOUND RD. P.O. BOX 13819 MILWAUKEE, WI 53213

In Australia Contact:
Hal Leonard Australia Pty. Ltd.
4 Lentara Court
Cheltenham, Victoria, 3192 Australia
Email: ausadmin@halleonard.com.au

Visit Hal Leonard Online at
www.halleonard.com

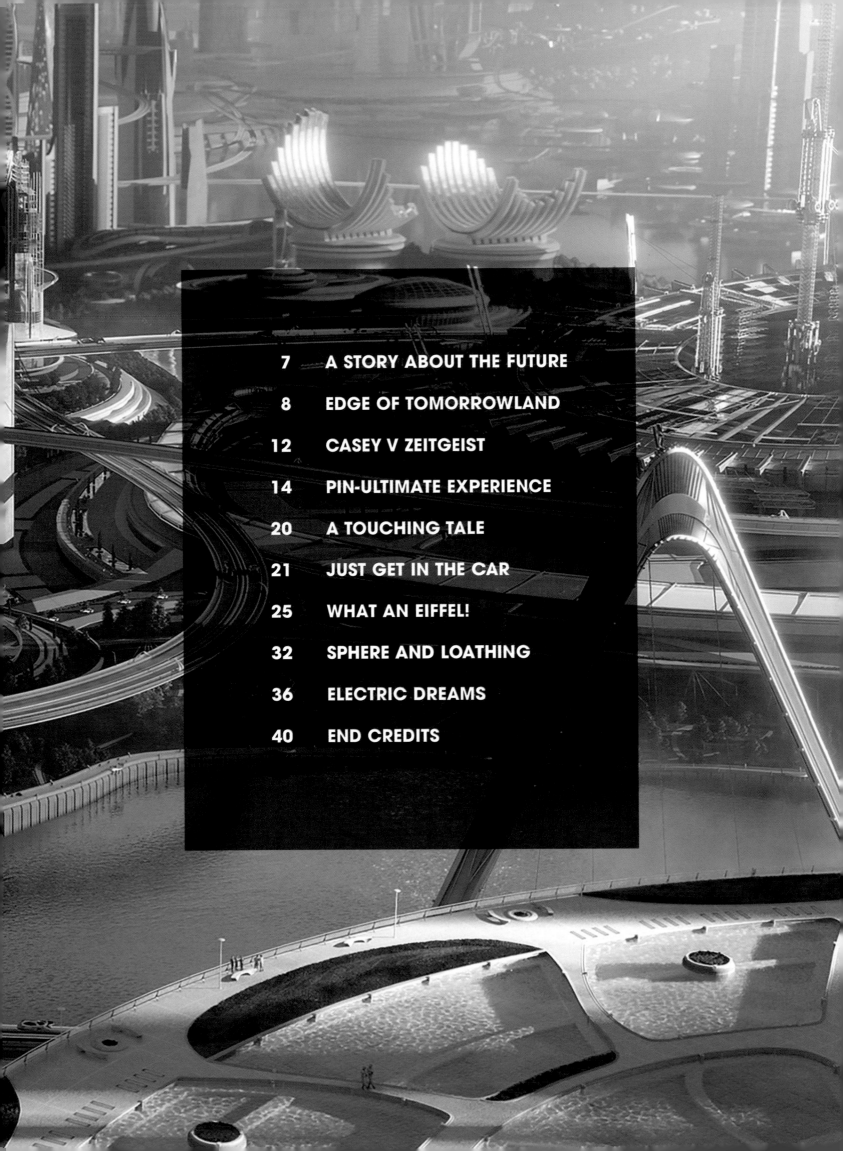

A STORY ABOUT THE FUTURE

Music by
MICHAEL GIACCHINO

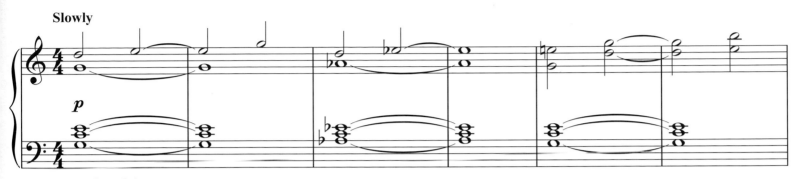

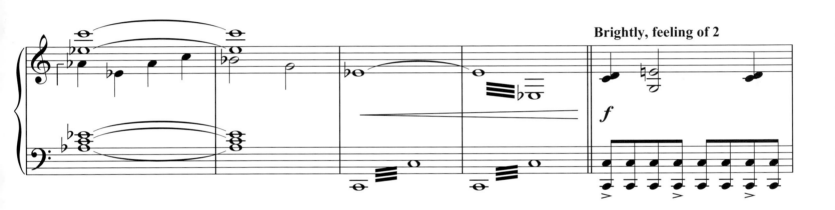

EDGE OF TOMORROWLAND

Music by
MICHAEL GIACCHINO

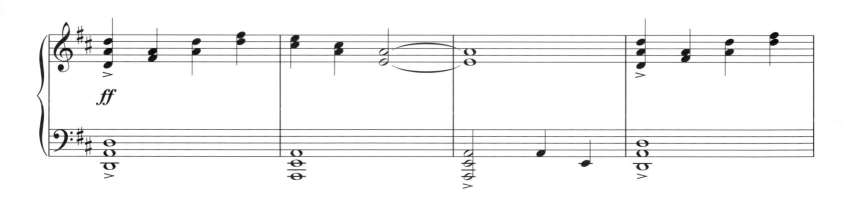

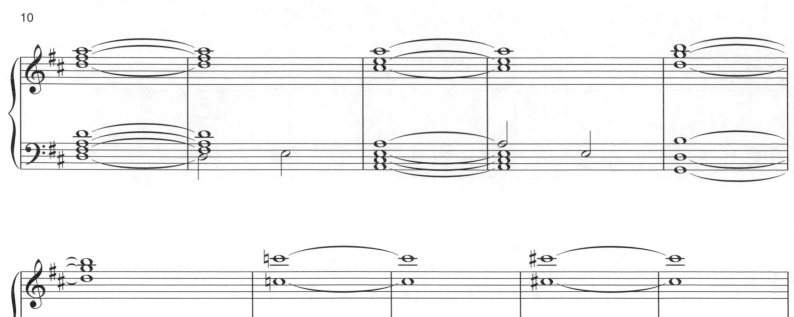

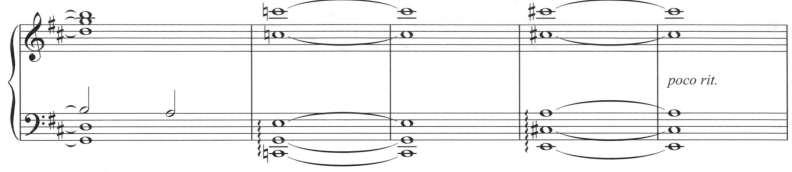

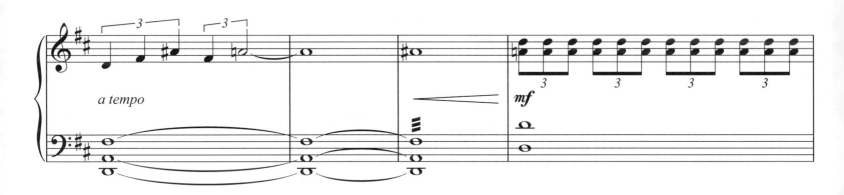

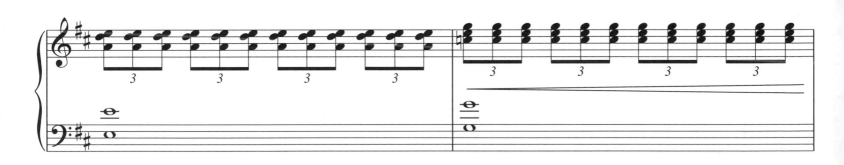

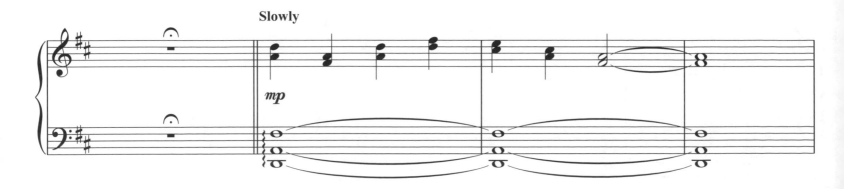

CASEY V ZEITGEIST

Music by
MICHAEL GIACCHINO

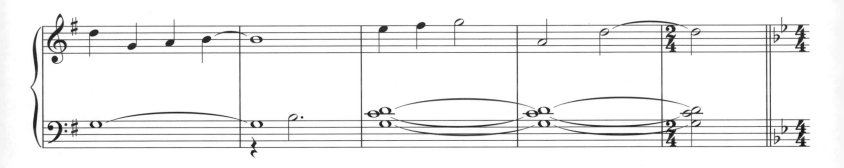

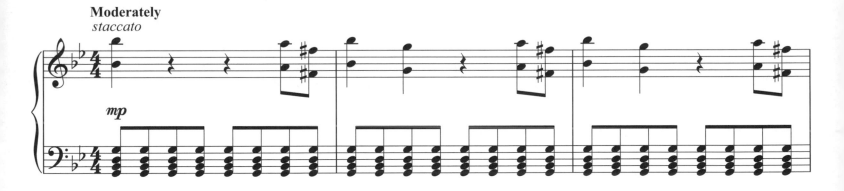

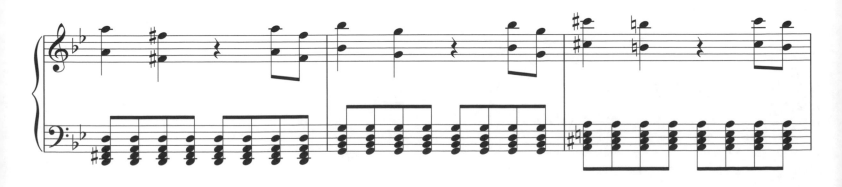

PIN-ULTIMATE EXPERIENCE

Music by
MICHAEL GIACCHINO

Moderately fast

With pedal

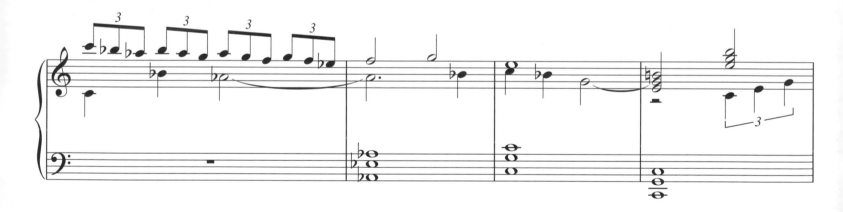

A TOUCHING TALE

Music by
MICHAEL GIACCHINO

Slowly and lyrically

JUST GET IN THE CAR

Music by
MICHAEL GIACCHINO

Quickly

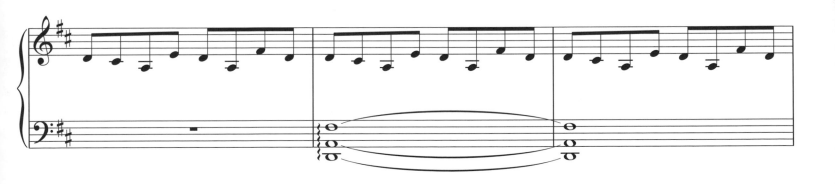

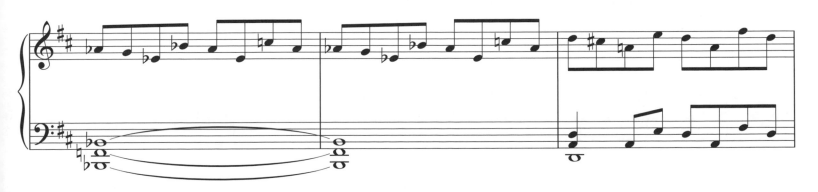

WHAT AN EIFFEL!

Music by
MICHAEL GIACCHINO

Moderately slow

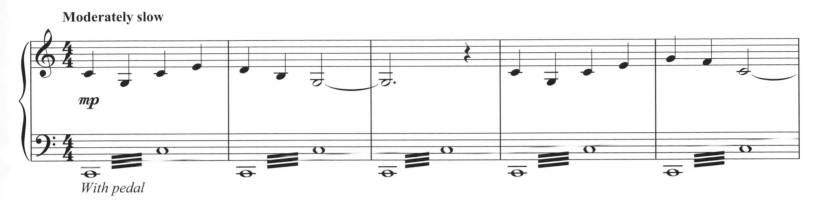

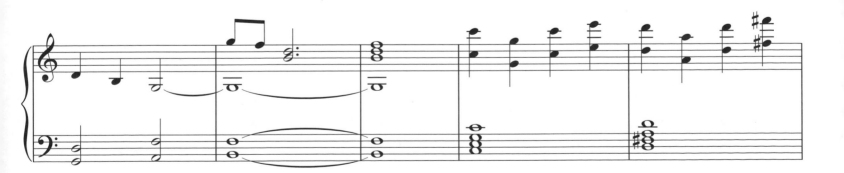

Brightly

Quickly

SPHERE AND LOATHING

Music by
MICHAEL GIACCHINO

Mechanistic Swing

ELECTRIC DREAMS

Music by
MICHAEL GIACCHINO

Slowly

END CREDITS

Music by
MICHAEL GIACCHINO

Brightly

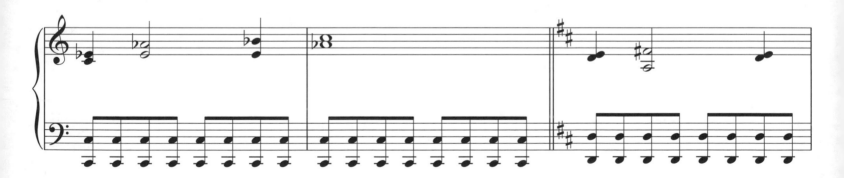